not a guide to

Liverpool

Dan Longman

First published 2012

The History Press
The Mill, Brimscombe Port
Stroud, Gloucestershire, GL5 2QG
www.thehistorypress.co.uk

British Library Cataloguing in Publication Data.
A catalogue record for this book is available from the British Library.

ISBN 978 0 7524 6884 6

Typesetting and origination by The History Press
Printed in Great Britain

Liverpool's coat of arms were granted in the year 1797. They depict a cormorant with a piece of seaweed in its beak, with a second bird placed on the crest. The gods of the sea Triton and Neptune are seen in support, holding banners displaying a third cormorant and a ship respectively. The importance of the sea is clear.

The cormorant is often referred to as the Liver Bird and its symbol has been used widely across the city. An early town seal showed the eagle of St John with a sprig of broom in its beak. This was *planta genista* and was the symbol of the royal house of the Plantagenets.

In 1644 the town seal was lost and a new one was made. The eagle was replaced by a cormorant, a more familiar bird in the area, and the piece of broom was replaced by seaweed.

The motto translates as 'God has given us this tranquillity'.

Contents

Liverpool

Pronounced /ˈlɪvəpuːl/)

The name is believed to originate from Liverpool's past geography, the city having originally been situated next to a pool or creek filled with thick and muddy water. This pool probably flowed into modern day Canning Place and Paradise Street and provided plenty of opportunities for the early maritime merchants to prosper.

Grid Reference

Royal Liver Building - 53° 24′ 20.88″ N, 2° 59′ 44.88″ W

Street Names

The correspondence of King John in 1207 reveals the exact moment when Liverpool was granted its Royal Charter. This allowed greater freedom to the town's inhabitants and sowed the seeds for its future prosperity. It was about this time when the city's original seven streets were first recorded and mapped out. These were:

Bank Street (now Water Street)
Castle Street
Chapel Street
Dale Street
Juggler Street (now High Street)
Moor Street (now Tithebarn Street)
Whiteacre Street (now Old Hall Street)

Some of the more unusual streets to be found in Liverpool include **Ranelagh Street**, named after an area of gardens that once existed on the present day site of the Adelphi Hotel. These were christened in homage to the well-to-do Ranelagh Gardens of Chelsea, London, at a time when Liverpool was reigning strong as second city of the empire. On the edge of the city centre stands **Byrom Street** which had at one time been known as Dog Kennel Lane, so-called because it was the location of the kennels of the city's official hunting dogs. Many of Liverpool's old Georgian streets have their origins in the slave trade, such as **Tarleton Street**. The Tarleton family made a great deal of money in the late eighteenth century, with no less than three generations involved in the practice. Their endeavours instigated over fifty foreign voyages, capturing thousands of slaves in the process.

Timeline

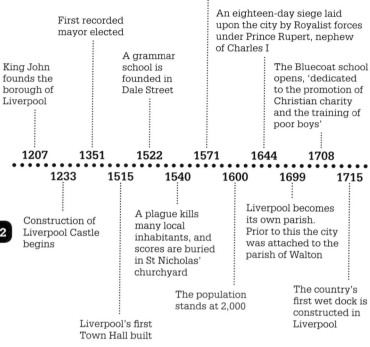

Locals present a petition to Queen Elizabeth describing themselves as 'inhabitants of Her Majesty's poor decayed town of Liverpool'.

An eighteen-day siege laid upon the city by Royalist forces under Prince Rupert, nephew of Charles I

First recorded mayor elected

A grammar school is founded in Dale Street

King John founds the borough of Liverpool

The Bluecoat school opens, 'dedicated to the promotion of Christian charity and the training of poor boys'

1207   1351   1522   1571   1644   1708

1233   1515   1540   1600   1699   1715

Construction of Liverpool Castle begins

A plague kills many local inhabitants, and scores are buried in St Nicholas' churchyard

Liverpool becomes its own parish. Prior to this the city was attached to the parish of Walton

The population stands at 2,000

The country's first wet dock is constructed in Liverpool

Liverpool's first Town Hall built

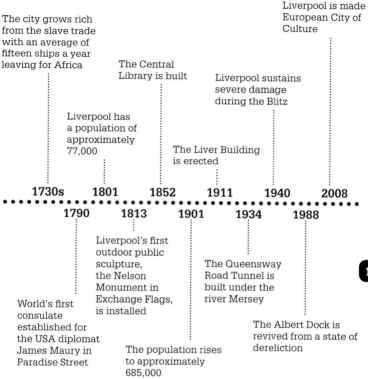

The city grows rich from the slave trade with an average of fifteen ships a year leaving for Africa

Liverpool is made European City of Culture

The Central Library is built

Liverpool sustains severe damage during the Blitz

Liverpool has a population of approximately 77,000

The Liver Building is erected

1730s   1801   1852   1911   1940   2008

1790   1813   1901   1934   1988

Liverpool's first outdoor public sculpture, the Nelson Monument in Exchange Flags, is installed

The Queensway Road Tunnel is built under the river Mersey

World's first consulate established for the USA diplomat James Maury in Paradise Street

The Albert Dock is revived from a state of dereliction

The population rises to approximately 685,000

Distance From

Place	Miles	Kilometres
Angkor Wat, Cambodia	10,135	6,298
Brussels, Belgium	578	359
Cairo Citadel, Egypt	3,796	2,359
Death Valley, USA	8,130	5,052
Eiffel Tower, France	630	392
Frankfurt, Germany	882	548
Gateshead Millennium Bridge, Newcastle	196	122
Hong Kong, China	9,687	6,019
Istanbul, Turkey	2,752	1,710
Jerusalem, Israel	3,876	2,409
The Kremlin, Russia	2,601	1,616
London, England	290	180
Mana Pools, Zimbabwe	8,541	5,308
Niagara Falls, North America	5,484	3,408
Osaka, Japan	9,459	5,878
Palermo, Italy	2,110	1,311
Queenstown, New Zealand	18,897	11,743
Reykjavik, Iceland	1,609	1,000
Sandefjord, Norway	1,034	643
The Taj Mahal, India	7,051	4382
Ural Mountains, Russia	4,189	2,603
Vatican City	1,721	1,069
Washington DC, USA	5,666	3,521
Xinyang, China	8,762	5,445
Yangambi, Democratic Republic of the Congo	6,622	4,115
Zacatecas, Mexico	8,808	5,474

My Liverpool

'I love Liverpool because of the diverse culture, the fantastic shopping experience and the fabulous nightlife, especially Mathew street. What I don't like is people stereotyping Liverpool people as thieves and scroungers.'
Linda Mee, support worker

'I don't like how mispronunciation has become the accepted norm. So many end their sentences with "you know warra mean like" and there's an over-use of the term "dead" to emphasise something. I overheard a lady greeting a friend and asking how she was. "I'm dead well" was her reply!'
David Owens, law advisor

'I like seeing the Liver Building every morning on my ten-minute journey into work (another good thing about Liverpool: no really awful rush hour). I also like the clutter and muddle of Bold Street, particularly walking down it around 6 p.m. when the shops are shutting and the working day is winding down.'
Joe Moran, lecturer

'I like the fab architecture and our splendid parks and open spaces. Then there's that amazing waterfront! I'm proud that so many well known artists and great people have come from and are associated with Liverpool.'
Ged Fagan, local historian

'I hate how the city centre always gets done up whilst most of the outskirts are forgotten about.'
John Singo, landscape gardener

'There is the strong sense of "togetherness" amongst the Liverpool people. It is this unique quality which enables Liverpudlians to embrace change, be it good or bad, and take it all in our stride.'
Les McCabe, job hunter

'The current influx of yuppie type out-of-towners taking on high profile decision-making positions annoys me as well as the years of financial neglect in our shipping and manufacturing industries.'
John Rex, electrician

'I love both the grandeur of the Anglican Cathedral and the unusual but striking design of the Metropolitan. I also love the fact that you can see twenty-five-year-old mothers out shopping wearing pyjamas, oversized rollers, sporting tattoos where their eyebrows used to be.'
Bob Edwards, civil servant

'I love the old architecture in the city but hate some of the new builds, like those black monstrosities at the pier head which have spoilt a lot of good views for photographers.'
Peter Craig, engineering foreman

'I love Liverpool for all the £1.70 a pint pubs and The Lobster Pot Chippy.'
Charlie Clarke, seaman

'I love the way when referring to siblings it's "our John" or "our Jean"... nobody else does this.'
Kathleen Faulkner, office assistant

'The wealth of museums here have plenty to offer in terms of history and culture, and there are loads of great places to eat, especially on the Albert Dock and around the pier head.'
Christopher George, medical editor

'Liverpool never ceases to surprise me. It's constantly evolving and adapting; reinventing itself to become one of the most famous cities in the world.'
Tracy Spargo, driving instructor

Town Twinnings

Cologne, Germany, since 1952

The isolation of Germany after the Second World War saw the country out in the cold. By extending the hand of friendship, Liverpool agreed to help forge new links between the two nations via this historic cultural connection.

Dublin, Ireland, since 1997

Liverpool has a strong Irish connection and many of its residents can claim Irish ancestry. The Dublin-born Lord Mayor Mike Black strived hard to carve out official recognition of this bond during his term of office, 1993-94.

Shanghai, China, since 1999

Shanghai and Liverpool are surprisingly similar and share many cultural and business aspirations. Both have an historic shipping trade, both have an iconic waterfront and both are key economic centres of their respective countries. The idea of twinning was happily accepted by both cities.

Rio De Janeiro, Brazil, since 2003

With an equally rich sporting heritage, these two cities were well matched to join up and highlight their common bonds. Rio is home to a number of sporting teams including Flamengo, the most supported club in the world. Their Millions Derby between Vasco de Gama and Flamengo is as fiercely contested as any Liverpool and Everton showdown.

Friendship links with other international cities

Givency les la Bassee (Belgium)

Halifax (Canada)

Havana (Cuba)

La Plata (Argentina)

Memphis (USA)

Minamitame-Cho (Japan)

Naples (Italy)

New Orleans (USA)

Odessa (Ukraine)

Ponsacco (Italy)

Ramnicu Valcea (Romania)

Valparaiso (Chile)

International Liverpools include:

Liverpool, New South Wales

Liverpool, Nova Scotia

Liverpool, Illinois

Liverpool, New York

Liverpool, Pennsylvania

Liverpool, Texas

East Liverpool, Ohio

Liverpool Beach, Antarctica

Freak Weather

In July 1833 fierce forks of lightning struck a towering windmill standing in Limekiln Lane. As the terrific thunderstorm raged on it severely damaged the mill's sails, cracked nearby paving flags and sent bricks sent flying out of an upper room of the mill and out into the street. That same night a dyehouse in Hood Street was also struck, shattering a wooden spout to pieces but causing no fatalities.

In 1891 children screamed in terror as lightning blazed down upon St Saviour's School at the corner of Crown Street and Canning Street. The building's spire was hit sending debris crashing down into the playground and into nearby houses. Elsewhere a boy named Johnson received burns to his face as he was sitting by the window watching the inclement weather: he was struck by lightning. Flood damage was widespread across the neighbourhood, and a man was electrocuted as he sailed on the river. He was killed outright.

Seriously stormy gales battered Liverpool in 1894 causing considerable damage to properties and injuring a number of people. Telegraph wires were ripped from their poles in Lord Street and could be seen thrashing about on the pavement. In Lime Street a horse was blown over bringing its carriage down upon an elderly man, breaking his leg in the process. The force of the wind even managed to lift Patrick Mulligan, who was riding on the top deck of a tram, onto the parapet of the North Western Hotel. He was shaken but unharmed by the incident.

The summer of 2010 saw flash floods wash over Merseyside as torrential rain poured from the skies. Numerous roads across the city were affected and several, including Aigburth Road, Queen's Drive and East Prescot Road, were closed for public safety. The Met Office stated that 14mm (0.5in) of rain fell in just one hour in Liverpool, with many residents forced to evacuate their homes.

Later that year Liverpool experienced its lowest temperatures since records began. The weather observation station based in Crosby, just north of the city, recorded a temperature of -17.5c on the cold winter's evening of 18 December of that year. Buses, flights and ferries were all affected by the blizzard, which saw 5in of snow fall in just a few hours.

A Day in the Life

06:00 – The sun rises over the glorious urban vista of the river Mersey

08:00 – Liverpool and Everton football players prepare for the afternoon's big game

10:00 – Shoppers begin to flock to the country's largest outdoor shopping centre, Liverpool One

12:00 – Chefs dish up delicious meals to hungry diners at the all-seeing Panoramic Restaurant

2:00 – The amphibious yellow duck tour bus plunges yet again into the waters of the Salthouse Dock

4:00 – The final lectures of the day begin for sleepy students at the city's universities

6:00 – Merseytravel transports passengers across the county as rush hour reaches its peak

8:00 – Actors at the Playhouse take their places as the curtain is about to rise

10:00 – Party-goers navigate the bustling bars of Matthew Street and Concert Square

How Many Times a Year

Do passengers pass through the terminals at John Lennon Airport?
5 million flying with five different airlines.

Do horses compete at Aintree Racecourse?
Seven times, including the world famous Grand National.

Does the Liverpool Arena and Conference Centre hold an event?
Over 200.

Do commuters depart from the Paradise Street interchange?
10 million, with twenty departures an hour.

Are visitors allowed to venture up to take in the evening views from the Anglican Cathedral?
Thirty-two, with views as far as Blackpool.

Does Liverpool host the famous Matthew Street Festival?
Just one, but it is the largest annual free music festival in Europe.

Does a vehicle travel through the Queensway Tunnel?
12.8 million, equal to 35,000 a day.

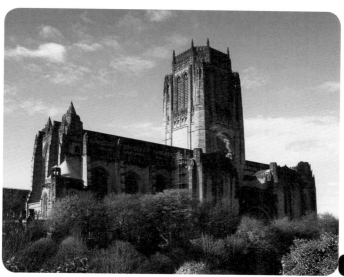

Demographics

As of 2001
Total number of residents – 439,473

Male – 209,805
Female – 229,668

Christian – 79.48 per cent
Muslim – 1.35 per cent
Buddhist – 0.27 per cent
Hindu – 0.26 per cent
Other – 0.13 per cent
No religion or not stated – 17.8 per cent

General health: Good – 64.47 per cent
General health: Fairly good – 21.74 per cent
General health: Not good – 13.79 per cent

Total number of full-time students – 28,659

Aged under 1 year – 4,835
Aged 100 years and over – 60

Strange Statistics

62 – The number of people who were hung at Walton Prison between 1887 and 1964.

35 tons – Each Mersey ferry holds this amount of fuel and burns a ton in 12 hours; they could travel across the Atlantic to New York without needing to refuel.

1838 – The year the first travelling post office ran between Liverpool and Manchester.

34th – This floor of the West Tower is home to the Panoramic Restaurant, Britain's tallest restaurant.

£125,203 – The average house price in Liverpool.

220ft high – The world's highest and heaviest ringing peal of bells can be found in the city's Anglican Cathedral. They weigh a combined total of 16.5 tons.

840 – Liverpool's census of 1272 returned this many listed residents.

1876 – The British public's second sight of a live gorilla took place this year at the William Brown Street Museum.

8.5 metres high – The world's largest fully robotic telescope was installed in the Canary Islands by Liverpool John Moores University in 2003. It has a 2-metre wide mirror which alone weighs over a ton.

800th – Liverpool celebrated this ancient birthday in 2007.

45,276 – Liverpool's home ground of Anfield has this level of seating whilst their rival's at Goodison Park can only accommodate 40,157.

18ft – The Liver Birds that sit upon the Royal Liver Building stand this tall and have a 24ft wingspan.

1 – Liverpool is officially the capital of pop. More artists with a Liverpool origin have had a number-one hit than anywhere else.

5,000 years old – The large stones of Calderstones Park are thought to be the oldest monuments in Liverpool: they date back to Neolithic times.

450 – The number of miles within the city boundaries by 1918.

Quotations Through History

'Lyrpole, alias Lyverpoole, a pavid towne, hath but a chapel... The king hath a castelet there, and the Earl of Darbe hath a stone howse there. Irisch merchants cum much thither, as to a good haven... At Lyrpole is smaul custom payed, that causith marchantes to resorte thither. Good marchandis at Lyrpole, and much Irish yarrn that Manchester men do buy there...'
John Leland, *Itinery, c.* 1536–39

'I know this by experience, that they are the most perfidious knaves to their landlords in all England; therefore I charge you, never trust them.'
Sir Edward Moore in a letter describing the Liverpool populace, 1667

'Liverpoole is one of the wonders of Britain... In a word, there is no town in England, London excepted, that can equal it for the fineness of the streets, and the beauty of the buildings.'
Daniel Defoe, *A tour thro' the Whole Island of Great Britain*, 1721–26

'One of the neatest, best towns I have seen in England.'
John Wesley, journal, 1755

'That immense city which stands like another Venice upon the water... where there are riches overflowing and everything which can delight a man who wishes to see the prosperity of a great community and a great empire.... This quondam village, now fit to be the proud capital of any empire in the world, has started up like an enchanted palace even in the memory of living men.'
Baron Erskine, 1791

'I have heard of the greatness of Liverpool but the reality far surpasses my expectation.'

Prince Albert, speech, 1846

'Liverpool… has become a wonder of the world. It is the New York of Europe, a world city rather than merely British provincial.'
***Illustrated London News*, 15 May 1886**

'Liverpool is the "pool of life".'
Carl Gustav Jung, *Memories, Dreams, Reflections*, 1928

'Liverpool has meant everything to me from the very beginning.'
Libor Pesek KBE, conductor, Liverpool Philharmonic, 1995

'The magic of Liverpool is that it isn't England. We are global and we have learned to tolerate and respect each other's traditions. As such, we are a national asset.'
Margaret Simey, political campaigner, 1999

'Liverpool will become a cultural beacon of the world. Capital of Culture is a wonderful accolade. It is fabulous. You are a wonderful city.'
Tessa Jowell, Culture Secretary, 2003

Famous For

The Waterfront

One of the most celebrated settings in Liverpool is the Pier Head, renowned for the Royal Liver Building, the Cunard Building and the Port of Liverpool Building. These are collectively referred to as the Three Graces and are recognised as being iconic symbols of the city's great nautical past. They are regarded by many as contributing to one of the most impressive waterfronts in the world and have been listed by UNESCO as a World Heritage Site.

Humour

Liverpool is known for its excellent sense of humour and many top comedians have hailed from the city over the years. Ken Dodd, Les Dennis, Tom O'Connor, Jimmy Tarbuck and John Bishop are but a few of the many who have helped keep Britain smiling.

The Beatles

World-renowned musicians who wowed the world in the 1960s. They went on to become one of the most acclaimed bands in history. The Beatles remain the best-selling band in the history of popular music, and over forty years after their break-up their recordings are still in high demand. They have had more number-one albums in the UK charts and have held the top spot longer than any other musical act to date.

Scouse

Scouse is a type of stew originally known as *lobscouse* or *lapskaus*, Norwegian for 'stew'. This refers to the meat based dish commonly eaten by sailors throughout Northern Europe which was popular in seaports such as Liverpool. Scouse is still a popular dish in the city, where it is a staple of local pub grub, although recipes vary greatly. 'Scouse' eventually came into common usage to describe the local accent of Liverpool and its residents as 'Scousers'.

Football

The city is home to two premiership football teams: Liverpool and Everton. Everton was founded in 1878 as a pastime for the people of St Domingo's parish. As the team developed, internal disputes arose resulting in the founding of a new team, Everton Athletic, in 1892. Later that year the name was changed to Liverpool FC, and soon the city had two impressive and competitive teams within its boundaries. Everton have played more top-flight league games than any other English team but Liverpool are close to being the most successful club in the history of English football. They are second only to the mighty Manchester United.

The Mersey Ferries

The famous Mersey Ferries actually originate from the town of Birkenhead on the other side of the river. Benedictine monks based at Birkenhead Priory had originally offered safe passage across the waters to travellers wishing to attend the markets that once took place in Liverpool. Back then Liverpool was only a small fishing village but nowadays thousands of visitors climb aboard the ferries each year in order to take in the unique views of the maritime metropolis and her waterfront attractions.

Infamous For

The Big Dig

The Big Dig was the name given to a series of building projects that took place in the run up to Liverpool's Capital of Culture year. Designed to modernise infrastructure in the city, the planning of the scheme was generally seen to have been a poor and an ill-managed mess. A 2008 survey by the *Liverpool Daily Post* reported some dire revelations: 80 per cent of city-centre users believed business to have suffered thanks to the Big Dig and only 32 per cent believed the work to have been worth the travel problems caused. Today the traffic chaos has finally subsided and the city flows happily once again. The journey here, however, has indeed been a stressful headache for many.

Public Pyjamas

It is not uncommon to catch sight of certain women of the neighbourhood dressed only in their pyjamas as they go about their days across various parts of the city. This appalling minority fashion trend has caused some heated debate between social commentators and has even spread to other parts of the country and even abroad. Opinions are truly divided over this curious issue, with Dr Helen Churchill of John Moores University quoted as saying, 'The interesting question isn't why people wear pyjamas, but why other people think it's a problem to do so. After all, they can be warm and practical. We should celebrate the wearing of pyjamas in public.' Others consider the notion to be thoroughly lazy and unhygienic and not the image this modern vibrant city should be portraying.

The Toxteth Riots

Back in 1981 an inner-city suburb of Liverpool known as Toxteth hit the headlines when rioting broke out after long-standing tensions between the black community and police. Bedlam broke out after the arrest of one individual and soon the area resembled a battleground. Pitched encounters between police and youths flooded the streets as petrol bombs and paving stones were launched through the air. The carnage last for nine whole days, during which 68 police officers were injured, 500 people arrested, 70 buildings destroyed and many cars burnt out. An official report (although primarily directed at the Brixton troubles of the same year) recognised that the riots represented an urgent need to tackle social problems such as poverty and deprivation that were rife in 1980s Merseyside.

Stereotypes

The people of Liverpool are successfully burying the old stereotypes and are laying the foundations for a decidedly reputable future. The days of the work-shy, tracksuited and moustachioed Scouser are dead and have been replaced by an image of a modern, technologically-savvy businessman and the hardworking all-rounder, both helping to drive their cherished city into a fresh new era. Liverpool now has a worldwide reputation for culture and the arts, with tourists flocking to the city's catalogue of museums. Liverpool is also becoming a safer city: the Home Office National Crime Statistics and the British Crime Survey (the two biggest indicators of crime levels in the country) show that there were 12,000 fewer victims on Merseyside in 2010 when compared to the previous year.

Making the Headlines

3 December 2007

The coveted Turner Prize was held at the Liverpool Tate in December 2007, the first venue outside of London in the event's twenty-three year history. It was won by the artist Mark Wallinger, whose display at the Turner Prize show was *Sleeper*, a film of him dressed in a bear costume wandering around an empty museum. However, the prize was officially given to him for *State Britain*, which recreated all the objects in Brian Haw's anti-war display in Parliament Square, London.

7 April 2008

A foliage sculpture of Beatle Ringo Starr was beheaded after the drummer outraged city residents with his comments. That week Starr had publically stated that he missed nothing about his hometown of Liverpool since moving away. The remaining Beatles topiary figures were left unharmed.

6 November 2008

The MTV Music Awards took place at the Echo Arena and drew in millions of viewers from around the world. Hosted by the singing superstar Katy Perry, this was the fifteenth such event and featured numerous big names including Pink, Kanye West, Take That and The Killers.

19 July 2011

The Museum of Liverpool finally opened its doors to the public after three years of construction. At a cost of £72 million it is expected to draw in crowds of 750,000 visitors a year. It broke records on its opening day as visitor numbers topped 12,000. At its peak there were 2,000 people coming through the Mann Island museum's doors every hour, putting the building in very good stead to reach its annual target.

28 July 2011

Families moved into the famous Brookside Close cul-de-sac eight years after the TV soap was axed. At the height of its popularity, *Brookside* regularly attracted 8 million viewers who witnessed everything from a patio burial to British television's first pre-watershed lesbian kiss. The properties are located in West Derby, a north-eastern suburb of Liverpool, and had sat empty for a number of years until they were bought and developed by a local businessman in December 2008.

Letters to the Press

One of the earliest and most tongue-in-cheek letters ever sent to the *Liverpool Mercury* hints at some questionable changes set to befall the city and proves that good old Scouse humour has existed for centuries.

Friday 30 August 1811

Gentlemen,

Knowing the great interest you take in all that concerns 'the good old town of Liverpool', I am happy to inform you 'exclusively' of the following improvements, which I understand, on very good authority, are speedily to take place.

Lord Street to be narrowed, so that two carriages cannot possibly pass each other. The imminent risk which those run who at present make the *attempt,* and the daily accidents which occur render this improvement highly necessary. Some persons have advised the Corporation to erect a toll-gate at each end, to increase their funds, but this is not decided upon.

The *whole* of Castle Street to be occupied as a market place, instead of *nine-tenths* at present. This will prevent so much crockery being broken and so many basket women lamed – N.B. In consequence of the above improvements, persons in carriages may come up Button Street, through Rainford's Garden, Matthew Street, John Street and Dale Street, to the Town Hall – or any other way they can find.

The buildings on the west side of Castle Street to be brought six yards forward to show the Town Hall to greater advantage.

When the inhabitants are invited to a *Public Meeting* at the Town Hall constables to be stationed at the doors, to prevent one person out of three from entering; the courtroom being judiciously calculated to accommodate only a few.

A new Dock to be built at Otter's Pool for the convenience of the Merchants – this to be a secret till the Corporation and their friends have purchased the land.

The present Docks to be each widened three yards; the expense will be trifling, and each Dock will then contain at least four ships or more.

The Children to go to Chester to be confirmed, there being no Church in Liverpool strong enough to bear a Bishop.

To have two Parish Meetings in the year instead of one; by which means many persons will go to Church twice as often as they do at present, and may by degrees acquire some reverence for the place and refrain from quarrelling and blaspheming therein.

All the Town Clocks to strike at different periods, to remind the inhabitants of the lapse of time, and make them punctual in their engagements.

The Common Council to choose the Mayor without troubling the Freemen about it; either by tossing up, drawing cuts or odds-or-even.

Witnesses to be more effectually brow-beaten at our Sessions, to prevent a man's telling a straight-forward story and to make him swear to more than he knows – N.B. It has been suggested to have the *rack* introduced (against which there is no law, as applied to *witnesses*).

A standing Committee to be appointed to put Ladies out of countenance, as they pass the Athenaeum steps. Non to be eligible but minors and broken-down rakes.

The offices of Physician and Surgeon to the infirmary and Dispensary to be put up at auction. Practitioners of ten years standing and upwards to produce certificates of ability – this to be dispensed with in the case of strangers and young students.

The Ladies and Gentlemen's Baths to be thrown into one to prevent peeping.

All the Cows within two miles to be driven through the town three times a day instead of twice. If there is a bull with them so much the better.

No Butcher to drive Calves through the streets without three Dogs to each Calf, instead of two as practiced at present. They will pass more quickly along, and by being well blooded the meat will be whiter.

The Gardener at the Mount to shut the Gardens more frequently during the day when people expect to be gratified with a walk therein. By their being more difficult of access, we shall be more sensible of their beauties.

The use of Knowsley Flags to be forbidden as they take from the peculiarity of our foot-pavements which is remarked by all strangers.

Five bells to be rung on Change instead of one; to put an end to impertinent conversation, and send Gentlemen home to their dinners.

The spire of St. Thomas's Church to be taken down. It is the only thing of the kind in the town, and looks singular.

I hope the above will appear to you to be judicious alterations, and remain yours, & Co.

Christopher Crab

Rebellious Liverpool

It has been said that the Liverpool general transport strike of 1911 was the closest time Britain has ever come to experiencing a full-blown revolution. The summer of that year brought city commerce to a standstill when over 60,000 men ceased work to take industrial action and harnessed the epic power of trade unionism. The rebellion had its roots in a sailor's strike of June of that year when merchant seaman successfully argued for better pay and conditions. Soon workers ranging from warehouse labourers to railway staff, all spurred on by activist Tom Mann, walked out of their jobs. Thousands of extra policemen and soldiers were brought to the city to control the crowds, many of whom had gathered at St George's Plateau on 14 August. It was there that mass riots broke out and inevitable violence culminated into a vicious day of unrest. This became known as Bloody Sunday. The strike lasted until 24 August when a deal was struck between staff and employees.

Tom Mann would later make an emotive speech stating that 'neither ship-owners nor reactionary committees nor councils, railway magnates, nor any other section shall be able to demoralise us again or drive us into poverty.'

Another major strike to take place in the city was carried out by Liverpool's very own police force. In 1919 the National Union of Police and Prison Officers called a strike after the Government voted through an act preventing such unionist measures by police. At the time many officers felt their jobs to be more difficult than that of a labourer with a wage just as bad. A labourer could expect an income of £3 7s a week whereas a policeman's pay packet could be as low as £2 3s, with long and tiring hours. Constables were on duty nearly eighty hours a week. Over 600 officers refused to work and were given a deadline of 8 p.m. to return to their beats or face the sack (London officers who went on strike were

immediately dismissed from duty). In all, over 900 policemen from Liverpool went on to hang up their handcuffs, almost 51 per cent of the overall force. Tanks, soldiers and even a battleship arrived in Liverpool to control public rioting and many special constables were drafted in to try and restore order. Several weeks into the rebellion virtually all striking officers had been replaced by men from outside the area and support for the action was beginning to die down. The strike cost the city over £125,000 in expenses under the Riot Damages Act. Despite the apparent failure of the strike, police staff later received pay increases and successive Governments finally began to take real notice of an officer's working conditions.

More recently students have taken to the streets to protest against rises in university tuition fees; nearly 2,000 academics have raised a placard in protest. Students from Liverpool's universities and prospective students from colleges and schools gathered at the Liverpool Guild of Students in Mount Pleasant on 24 November 2010. Some demonstrators staged sit-down protests in Lime Street and at the top of Bold Street, blocking traffic on a number of city-centre roads. Chanting crowds also marched towards Liverpool ONE before being dispersed by waiting police. This was just one march of many that took place across Britain in an effort to persuade the Government to cancel plans to allow universities to charge up to £9,000 per annum for courses. This was not achieved and now both Liverpool John Moores and Liverpool University charge the maximum rate whilst Liverpool Hope University charges £8,250 to students for their education.

Buildings: the Best

St George's Hall

The wonderfully Neoclassical St George's Hall is Grade I listed and was once home to the city's law courts as well as a large and luxurious concert room. The site was formerly occupied by an infirmary which had stood on the site since the early 1700s. However, in 1836 it was agreed that Liverpool needed something new. Harvey Lonsdale Elmes won the right to design the hall and his construction began in 1838. Elmes died of consumption seven years into the project, so emergency engineers were called in until Sir Charles Cockerell finished the job in 1854. Today the hall is one of Liverpool's greatest and most regal buildings and is used for a variety of special occasions throughout the year.

The Royal Liver Building

The Royal Liver Building was built in 1911 as the headquarters of the insurance specialists the Royal Liver Group. The business was first established in 1850 as the Liverpool Lyver Burial Society which was set up to provide respectable internments for its deceased members and to help their remaining families. The building's clock faces are the biggest in Britain and its hands are even bigger than Big Ben's. They were also known as George Clocks as they started at the exact moment King George V was crowned on 22 June 1911. Above sit two giant Liver Birds; legend has it that if the Liver Birds were ever to fly away, the city would cease to exist. The Liver Building still remains the most iconic of designs that Liverpool has to offer and is distinctly recognisable the world over.

The Town Hall

The first known Town Hall for Liverpool was built in the early sixteenth century and was little more than a barn with a thatched roof. As Liverpool grew in size and importance, a new town hall was ordered. In 1673 the new hall opened for business. It was known as the Exchange due to the inclusion of a ground-floor trading area for merchants and market traders to carry out their mercantile business. In 1748 a third town hall was commissioned in the grandest Georgian style. Over its lifetime the building has undergone a number of alterations and happily survived several fires, riots, canon fire and even a Fenian bomb plot. Today the council's ninety members meet every seven weeks to discuss the city's affairs and debate local politics in the hall's oak and mahogany Council Chamber inside this impressive-looking development.

St John's Beacon

Also known as the Radio City Tower, this unusual structure is home to an eponymous radio station. The tower had been built in 1969 and was not meant to be a permanent structure: it was designed as a ventilation shaft for the construction of St John's Market. It went on to become a revolving restaurant before DJs took over in the year 2000. It now houses the station's offices, studios and a public observation level from where some of the best views of Merseyside are to be had. At 138 metres high it is currently Liverpool's second tallest structure.

Buildings: the Worst

The Royal Liverpool University Hospital

The Royal Liverpool University Hospital is a grotesque concrete mess that should never have been given the go ahead. In a recent poll this was rightly voted as the city's worst building with a sorry local commenting, 'It's a disgrace, an eyesore. You would have to be ill to go there voluntarily. It looks like a prison. I feel sorry for anyone having to go there... and I'm a nurse!' This monstrosity was constructed between 1966 and 1978 and contains more than fifty wards. It has the largest accident and emergency department in the country. It is hoped that plans drawn up to redevelop the hospital will be set in motion in the very near future.

The Metropolitan Cathedral

The Metropolitan Cathedral was recently named by American news network CNN as one of the ugliest buildings in the world. They stated, 'far from conjuring images of heavenly repose, the church is more akin to a giant concrete tent, hence its local nickname "Paddy's Wigwam" (Paddy being pejorative for Catholics of Irish descent).' It was built in Hope Street in 1967 to a design that is certainly unique, but many consider there to be far worse structural offenders plaguing the city skyline.

The Capital Building

In New Hall Place stands a brutish beige construction officially known as the Capital Building. This was completed in 1974 by the Royal & Sun Alliance as one of their numerous UK bases and contains thirteen floors of office space. It has become known locally as the Sandcastle due to its sandy shades but fails to impress when set against an otherwise architecturally-pleasing urban landscape.

St John's Market and The Holiday Inn

This dastardly duo certainly deserves to be demolished. They stand on Lime Street greeting passengers from the station with a drab and appalling first impression. The market was opened in 1971 and paying a visit today is like stepping through a time warp. The precinct feels out of date and permeates an almost shabby atmosphere completely out of touch with the rest of modern Liverpool. The Holiday Inn sits like a decaying Lego block appearing to have just been dropped on top of the market and left to rot. In 2008 reports appeared in the local press regarding designs for a brand new multimillion-pound upgrade to the properties on this site. These proposals suggested that the market would be vastly updated with improved natural lighting throughout and the addition of a new food terrace overlooking Clayton Square. Whether these exciting plans will get the go-ahead is not yet known, but they would certainly bring this part of town back up to par.

Historic Miscellany

In 1903 Bootle proudly rejected plans to be incorporated into the city of Liverpool and chose to remain governed under its own authority. This went against previous trends which had seen areas such as Wavertree, West Derby, Walton, Toxteth and Garston succumb to Liverpudlian control in the late nineteenth century.

One of Britain's earliest steam rollers was set to work on the streets of Liverpool after officials were impressed by road quality in the thoroughfares of Paris. Acquired in 1867 at a cost of £700, it was known locally as the 'Demon Crusher'.

In 1849 the pregnant Ann Henrichson was brutally murdered along with her two infant children and a servant at a house in Leveson Street. The culprit was later hanged. However, in the January of 1850 the property was converted into a public house where drinkers could enjoy a glass whilst marvelling at the very scenes where the atrocities took place. The building no longer stands and the street is now known as Grenville Street South.

Britain's only ever Prime Minister to be assassinated, Spencer Percival, was gunned down by Liverpool-born John Bellingham in 1812.

Keeper Richard Howard was crushed to death by Rajah the elephant at the zoological gardens in 1844. His body was mortally fractured when the animal pinned him up against the iron bars of the enclosure.

In 1913 militant suffragette Edith Rayner planted a bomb at the Liverpool Cotton Exchange. It failed to explode.

Liverpool MP William Huskisson became the world's first railway fatality when mortally wounded by Stephenson's *Rocket* on the opening day of the Liverpool to Manchester railway in 1830.

World-renowned entertainer Charlie Chaplin was once a temporary pupil at the Liverpool's school of Saint Xavier at the turn of the last century.

Charles Dickens is said to have been made a special constable in Liverpool for one evening in the 1860s. He observed police as research for his novels.

PROLIFIC JOURNALIST, NOVELIST AND FOR...

CHARLES DICKENS
BORN PORTSEA 1812 · DIED GAD'S HILL, KENT 1870

SO WROTE DICKENS, WHOSE FIRST VISIT WAS IN 1838, FROM 1842 UNTIL
1869, HE WAS A FREQUENT VISITOR, GIVING READINGS FROM HIS
NOVELS, USUALLY TO LARGE AUDIENCES AT ST GEORGE'S
HALL, ALSO AT THE FORMER MASQUE THEATRE, DUKE
STREET IN 1860 HE WAS SWORN-IN AS A CONSTABLE
FOR RESEARCH PURPOSES'

PLAQUE UNVEILED 17 JANUARY 2004

..."ONE DAY IN 1860, LIVERPOOL POLICE CONSTABLE

71

Museums and Galleries

Liverpool is known for its cultural amenities, with plenty of fascinating museums and galleries on offer.

The Museum of Liverpool

The World Museum

The Walker Art Gallery

International Slavery Museum

Sudley House

National Conservation Centre

The Bluecoat

Liverpool War Museum

The Beatles Storey

Tate Liverpool

Victorian Gallery and Museum

The Williamson Tunnels Heritage Centre

St George's Hall

The Liverpool FC Tour and Museum

Merseyside Maritime Museum

INTERNATIONAL SLAVERY MUSEUM

Open daily 10am – 5pm

FREE ENTRY

NATIONAL MUSEUMS LIVERPOOL

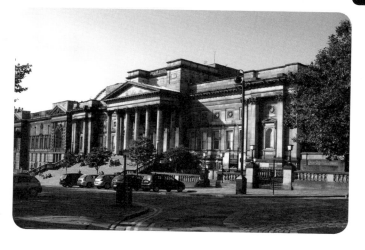

Parks and Green Spaces

Liverpool has plenty of parks for locals and visitors to escape the concrete jungle and take time to relax in greener surroundings, including:

St John's Gardens

Allerton Tower Park

Calderstones Park

Camp Hill

Princes Park

Otterspoool Park

Croxteth County Park

Everton Park

Newsham Park

Chavasse Park

Sefton Park

Stanley Park

Reynolds Park

St James' Gardens

Wavertree Park

Greenbank Park

Businesses

Liverpool is home to an array of home-grown businesses, and many of the High Street's familiar names have their origins in the city.

The Cains Brewery was founded by Robert Cain back in 1858. He had owned a small pub in Lime Kiln Lane (now Lime Street) and brewed his own ale on the side. With the commercial success of his beer, Robert was able to purchase a brewery based in Stanhope Street and he soon became known as a brewer of particular quality. Within twenty-five years he had established 200 pubs, the most famous being the Philharmonic Dining Rooms in Hope Street. By the time of his death in 1906 the brand of Cains was known the world over and Robert had been ennobled as Lord Brocket, making a vast fortune. The firm later merged with Walkers of Warrington thus becoming Walker Cains. Today the brewery is owned by Dusanj brothers who saved it from the brink of despair in 2008. Cains continues to thrive and remains a popular brand across the UK.

The Owen Owen firm was founded by Owen Owen, a Welshman who opened up his first drapery store in London Road in 1868. By 1900 Owen Owen had become one of the largest employers in the North West with 400 employees working in its shops. Over the years the business prospered, and a brand-new purpose-built department store was set up in Clayton Square and a merger with T.J. Hughes was agreed. The rejuvenated firm grew in popularity after a decline in sales during the 1920s before being sold off sixty years later. Recently T.J. Hughes went into administration: it was unable to pay its multimillion pound debts, with many job losses taking place. Out of its fifty-seven stores, only six could be saved by investors – but this does includes the firm's original flagship store in the historic London Road.

The White Star Line was a prominent shipping company famous for its most unfortunate vessel, *Titanic*. The original White Star Line had been forced into bankruptcy in the 1860s and the name was purchased by Thomas Ismay who set up headquarters in Albion House, James Street. Its main competitor was the Southampton-based Cunard Line, and in response to their grand cruisers of the *Lusitania* and *Mauretania*, Ismay ordered the building of the *Titanic*, *Britannic* and *Olympic*, the latter being the only ship of this class to make a profit. The two rivals later merged to form Cunard White Star and staff were moved out of the city down to new offices situated on the south coast. Today the liner is based near to London's Trafalgar Square and continues to operate luxury cruise liners for tourists and holidaymakers.

The bakery company of Sayers was founded in 1912, offering fresh produce to hungry Liverpudlians from Fred and Lillian Sayer's shop in Prescot Road, Old Swan. So successful was their venture that ten years later they moved to County Road, Walton, to bigger and better premises. Expansion continued and there are now over 100 stores operating across the north of England. The bakery remained a family-run business until 1977, when it was sold to United Biscuits and then again to Warburtons, owners of the fellow bakery chain of Hampsons, in 1990. It has since undergone several more management alterations, with some branches soon to evolve into Poundbakeries. Sayers is still the biggest independent retail baker in the Northwest.

Political Figures

William Gladstone

Born at No. 62 Rodney Street in 1809, William Gladstone became one of the most eminent politicians in history. He was educated at Eton and Oxford University and elected MP for Newark, Nottinghamshire, in 1832. He was a traditional Conservative of his time, opposing the abolition of slavery and factory legislation. In the 1840s, however, Gladstone began a mission to save London prostitutes from their clandestine trade and rehabilitate them for suitable employment, which resulted in harsh criticism from his well-to-do peers. Nevertheless, Gladstone flourished in the House of Commons and served as Chancellor a total of three times and as Prime Minister, four. Gladstone is both the oldest ever person to form a government – he was aged eighty-two at his final appointment – and the oldest person ever to occupy the Premiership – he was aged eighty-four upon his resignation. He died of heart failure in 1898 at his home of Hawarden Castle in North Wales. The William Gladstone pub in North John Street is named in his honour.

William Roscoe

One of the city's most well-respected sons was the merchant and MP William Roscoe. He was born at the Old Bowling Green House, a tavern on Mount Pleasant near what is now the corner of Hope Street. After working as a gardener with his father for several years he secured a job at a solicitor's, becoming a lawyer himself in 1774 and later an MP. William's tenure lasted just one year; he resigned his seat in 1807 but not until he had voted successfully in favour of abolishing slavery and several other altruistic bills. Roscoe is seen by many as the founder of Liverpool culture. A keen poet, writer, botanist and patron of the arts, he laid the foundations for Liverpool's future as one of the world's most creative destinations. Many streets laid in tribute can be found dotted around the city as can his numerous cultural collections, which are free to view inside Liverpool's multitude of museums and galleries.

WILLIAM ROSCOE, 1753 – 1831.
...TION OF THE LIVERPOOL, ROYAL INSTITUTION.

Bessie Braddock

Born in 1899, Elizabeth Braddock formally entered politics in 1930 when she became a city councillor for St Anne's Ward and later the leader of the Liverpool Trades Council. After serving as an ambulance assistant during the war, Bessie won the seat of Liverpool Exchange for the Labour Party in 1945, a position she held for twenty-four years, during which she fought for maternity, child welfare and youth issues. She was also a key figure in support for the flooding of Tryweryn valley in Wales. This was to create a reservoir of fresh water to supply homes in Liverpool. The motion was passed, and the entire village of Capel Celyn was flooded in 1965, forcing around seventy of its former inhabitants to find a new home. In 2005 the city formally apologised by issuing a statement acknowledging the 'insensitivity by our predecessor council'.

Scientific Discoveries

Toxteth-born astronomer Jeremiah Horrocks predicted and observed the transit of Venus of 1639. He died of unknown causes in 1641, aged only twenty-two. Horrocks Avenue in Garston is named after him.

Dr Matthew Dobson of the Liverpool Infirmary discovered a breakthrough in diabetes. In 1772 Dobson studied thirty-three-year-old diabetic Peter Dickonson and was the first to find that his urine contained remnants of sugar. He became president of the Liverpool Medical Library in 1779.

In the fight against 1830s cholera, Kitty Wilkinson opened her home to the public and used the only boiler in the street to wash clothes and linen. Kitty's idea worked, and public wash houses begin to open up across Britain. In 1846 Kitty was presented to Queen Victoria in recognition of her services to the city.

The Liverpool School of Tropical Medicine, the world's first, was founded in 1898 by Sir Alfred Lewis Jones. Over the years researchers have discovered many breakthroughs, such as the link between mosquitoes and malaria in 1902.

In 1896 Oliver Lodge became the first man to use x-ray photography in medicine by revealing a bullet in a boy's hand at Liverpool's Royal Southern Hospital in Caryl Street.

Crime and the Macabre

Towns and cities across the country are steeped in a wealth of criminal history. Liverpool is no different.

In April 1837 Daniel Cole was sentenced to transportation for life after he killed a police constable in Hanover Street. Officer Bailey had pursued Cole in connection with a domestic incident in nearby College Lane but was fatally stabbed in the neck during his struggle to make the arrest. Locals wrestled Cole to the ground and he was escorted to the Hotham Street, Bridewell, to await his fate. The deceased Constable Bailey left a wife and two children.

A lenient sentence was given to Mary Ann Crawley of Lonsdale Road, who received just one day's imprisonment after being found guilty of manslaughter. In the March of 1869 Mrs Crawley's husband had came home drunk and argumentative and became violent. In her defence, Mary grabbed a bottle of paraffin oil and launched it at her intoxicated spouse, setting him ablaze. He ran out screaming into the street and was soon attended by medics who conveyed him to hospital. He later died of lockjaw and Mary was luckily brought before a court that happened to sympathise with her actions.

It was a sad state of affairs that saw eighty-four-year-old Hannah Fitzgerald commit suicide by throwing herself from a Liverpool workhouse window in the January of 1870. She had been confined to the institution for some fifteen months and in that time her mental health had deteriorated, and she had often been found wandering around the corridors in the dead of night. Shortly before six o'clock on New Year's Day, workhouse staff found her limp and broken body in the institution's yard, some five stories below the open window of her ward.

On 1 July 1884 the body of fifty-nine-year-old Frances Wallace was found slumped in the water closet of her home at No. 22 Hope Place. A sanitary official discovered her decaying body and found it to be in an advanced state of decomposition, almost like a mummy. A later autopsy revealed swarms of dead bluebottles lying inside her skull. An open verdict was returned with doctors believing Mrs Wallace to have died from an apoplectic fit some time before.

A suicide took place in one city-centre pub when depressed and unemployed Duncan Owens entered Paradise Street's Beehive Hotel on 12 March 1898. The twenty-two-year-old requested a shot of whiskey and a glass of water before adding his own mysterious powder to the beverages. Owens then disappeared to the toilets, where he was later found keeled over on the floor. He confessed to poisoning himself with oxalic acid and died on the way to hospital shortly afterwards.

In February 1908 William Vaughn attempted to shoot solicitor James Alsop in his office at No. 14 Castle Street over a legal dispute. Two bullets were fired but one only reached its target and embedded itself in Alsop's arm. Vaughn was chased through the city and captured by police. He later received a sentence of five years' penal servitude for wounding in an attempt to kill.

Ghosts

Numerous ghost sightings have been recorded across Liverpool and it has been argued that the city may well be the most haunted in Britain.

One spectre said to walk Rodney Street is the ghost of William McKenzie, the top-hatted spirit of a Victorian businessman. His tomb is located in the grounds of St Andrew's and baffles many visitors with its bizarre architectural form. It was erected in 1868 and built of granite in the shape of a small pyramid. McKenzie's skeletal remains allegedly sit above ground at a table so that the Devil may not claim his soul.

There have been reports that the Playhouse Theatre in Williamson Square features a spook that haunts the building after tragedy struck in 1896. It was on Boxing Day that year that fifty-two-year-old Mary Elizabeth Edmondson was accidently killed when a fire curtain came down and struck her on the head. The curtain, which weighed about a ton and was made of iron and asbestos, was approximately 4ft from the ground and had been partially raised so that Mary could clean the stage. Confusion between stage hands caused the rope that supported the heavy curtain to be lowered and the incident was officially recorded as an accident. Her ghost is said to haunt the theatre's gallery level.

Aintree Racecourse is said to be haunted by horses that have long since perished. In 2008 a report appeared in the *Liverpool Echo* featuring claims from a stable manager who believed he had seen, on several occasions, a grey horse walking around the yard at night. He also said that at other times he had noticed another trot about the course near the stands before vanishing before his very eyes.

The infamous Spring-Heeled Jack, a mysterious figure that could breathe fire and jump inhuman distances, was spotted in Liverpool in the late nineteenth century. People who claimed to have seen him gave truly terrifying descriptions of a frightful appearance with diabolical physiognomy, clawed hands and eyes that 'resembled red balls of fire'. Legend has it that he jumped from the church tower of St Francis Xavier's in Langsdale Street without any injury.

Croxteth Hall may well be home to the spirit of previous owners and has recently been the scene of an investigation by paranormal researchers. In 2009 a luminous yellow glow was captured on CCTV and can be seen emerging from trees outside the hall. It heads up the path towards the house before disappearing.

Liverpool at War

The Blitz

Liverpool and the surrounding area suffered extensive damage during the bombing raids of the Second World War and towns on both sides of the Mersey came under fierce aerial attack. This was the most bombed location outside of London due to the important shipping industries based on its shores. The May Blitz of 1941 resulted in intense losses and numerous injuries, with the destruction of many of the area's railways, docks, factories and residential streets. In total, the German air raids brought deaths to approximately 4,000 of Merseyside's inhabitants and left the city plagued with dreadful memories for many years after.

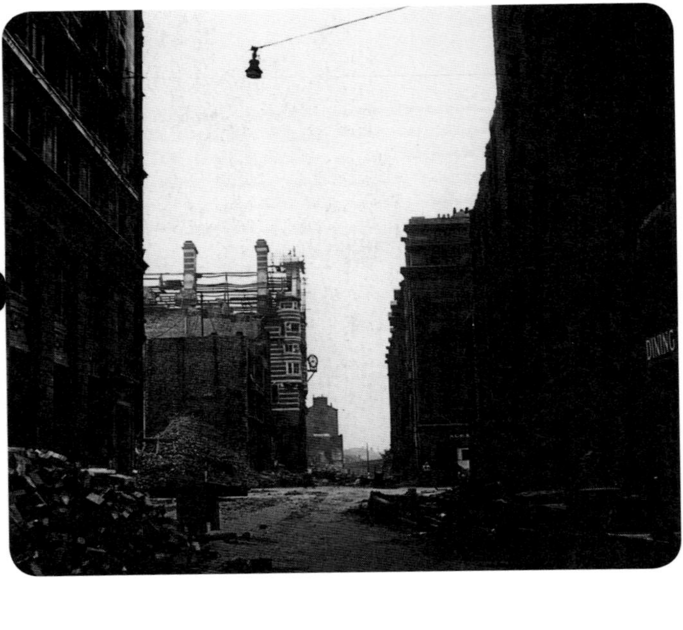
DINING

Notable Alumni

Dame Stella Rimington studied archive administration at Liverpool University in the late 1950s. She later became the first female Director General of the British intelligence agency MI5.

Beth Tweddle attended Liverpool John Moores and is considered by many to be Britain's most successful gymnast of all time. She completed her degree in Sports Science in 2007.

Honorary fellows at Liverpool John Moores include the comedian Ken Dodd, actress Kim Cattrall, footballer Stephen Gerrard, playwright Willy Russell and his Holiness the Dalai Lama.

A Scene to See

A Scene to Miss

Festivals

The city is host to the world famous Matthew Street Festival and it currently holds the title for being the largest free annual music festival in the whole of Europe. The last event in 2011 saw approximately 160,000 music fans visit Liverpool to celebrate the festival's eighteenth birthday as six outdoor stages played host to a multitude of musical entertainment.

Creamfields is a popular festival that focuses heavily on dance music, and it is one of the most renowned events in the UK music calendar. The British line-up is now held every year in Daresbury, Cheshire, but its early origins lie in Liverpool. Since 1999 Creamfields has established itself as the crown jewel of dance festivals and continues to be in the top five festivals alongside the likes of Glastonbury, V and Reading.

More music comes from the city's Sound Festival, a hugely respected three-day international music, media and technology extravaganza packed with live arts and gigs.

Merseyside's strong Irish connections warrant the city to hold an official Irish Festival each year. The festival provides visitors with entertainment and education in Irish traditions, music, literature, theatre, and art, and highlights their significance in defining Liverpool's culture as it continues to prosper as a major world city.

Liverpool Pride is a relatively new addition to city's event list after parading for the first time in 2010. It attracted an audience of over 21,000 and took place around the city's 'Gay Quarter' with stages on Dale Street, Exchange Flags and North John Street. Organisers hailed the festivities as a massive success and now plan to hold even larger events in the future. 2011 saw visitor numbers double to over 40,000, with future marches set to be just as popular.

Musicians

Liverpool is a city of talented musicians and many a great act has hailed from its streets. Some of its more noteworthy acts of past and present include:

The Searchers – Part of the 1960s 'Merseybeat' scene, their biggest hit was 'Needles and Pins', which reached number one in the charts in 1964.

The Wombats – This indie-rock group have a large fan base amongst Britain's younger generation, with their biggest hit to date, 'Moving to New York', peaking at number eleven in the UK singles charts. The band had the honour of being the opening act at Liverpool's Capital of Culture ceremony in 2008, and their track 'Let's Dance To Joy Division' was awarded 'Best Dancefloor Filler' at the NME Awards.

Billy Fury – An internationally successful singer from the late-1950s to the mid-1960s, his hits included 'Jealousy', 'When Will You Say I Love You?' and 'Last Night Was Made for Love'.

Cilla Black – Born Priscilla White in 1943, she racked up a series of hits such as 'Anyone Who Had a Heart', and 'You're My World'. She also enjoyed a thriving TV career and was later known for her role as the host of *Blind Date*.

The Zutons – With top ten hits including 'Why Won't You Give Me Your Love?' and 'Valerie' (the latter covered by Mark Ronson and Amy Winehouse), The Zutons are now an established name on the indie-rock music scene.

Frankie Vaughan – Known as 'Mr Moonlight' after an early hit, Vaughan specialised in US covers. He reached the top of the charts in 1957 with 'The Garden of Eden' and again in 1961 with 'Tower of Strength'.

The Beatles – World-renowned kings of music, Paul, George, John and Ringo achieved legendary status with their catalogue of hits across the globe. The band achieved seventeen number-one hits on the Record Retailer singles chart between May 1963 and July 1969. In the USA they had a total of twenty number-one singles between February 1964 and June 1970. 'I Want to Hold Your Hand', 'Paperback Writer' and 'Eight Days a Week' are just some of the bands best loved tunes.

The La's – With their heyday in the 1980s and '90s, The La's most famous single 'There She Goes' reached number thirteen in the UK Charts in 1990.

Frankie Goes to Hollywood – This 1980s dance pop group caused controversy with their debut single 'Relax' when it was banned by the BBC. This act ultimately pushed the track to the top of the charts and it became the seventh best selling song to date. After the follow-up success of 'Two Tribes' and 'The Power of Love', they became only the second act in the history to reach number one with their first three singles, the first being fellow Liverpudlians Gerry & the Pacemakers in 1964.

Local Lingo

For those outside the area the Scouse accent can be a little difficult to get to grips with. Some of the more unusual phrases locals may use are:

Antwakky – Old fashioned

Beast – Great

Bevvie – A drink

On me Bill – Alone

Bizzies – The police

Chokka – Very busy

Class, Sound or Laughin – Good or I like it

Cob on – To sulk or be unhappy

Come ed – Come on

Deffo – Certainly

Divvy – Stupid person

Fit – Attractive

Geg – To be nosy

Happenin' la? – How are you?

Iffy – Strange

In a bit – Goodbye

Is right – I agree

Kecks – Pants or underwear

Kidda or La – Friend

Made up – Pleased

Messy – Drunk

No mark – someone of no importance

Over the water – The Wirral

Scally – Chav or mischievous character

Scran – Food

Shady – Unfair

Town – City centre

Us – Me

Woolyback or Plazzy Scouser – A person from a town near to but not Liverpool itself

Ya ma – Your mother

Youz – You lot

Liverpool on Television

Liverpool has been the location of choice for a number television shows and films.

Z-Cars was a 1960s and '70s drama series based in the fictional town of Newtown, which itself was based on Kirby, a suburb on the outskirts of Liverpool. The programme's plots dealt with the lives of police officers and the associated aspects of the profession. Social realism and interesting stories endeared its characters to the general public.

The Liver Birds ran from 1969 to 1978 and concentrated on the problems encountered by two young single women when dealing with boyfriends, work, parents and friendship.

The Onedin Line was a historical drama set in Liverpool between the years 1860 to 1886. It focused on the fictional business of James Onedin and his shipping company. It ended in 1980 after a run of eight series.

Boys from the Black Stuff was a 1980s drama by Alan Bleasdale which chronicled the lives of a group of Liverpool labourers as they sought to find work against a backdrop of suffering during the infamous Thatcher years. The series was critically well-received and was seen as a valid reflection of the real struggles faced by the northern working class of the day.

The sitcom *Bread* ran from 1986-91 and again portrayed the difficulties of a typically Catholic Liverpool family of the time and the ways they sought to secure a comfortable lifestyle.

Brookside, a long-running soap opera for Channel 4, was set in Liverpool and was the brainchild of Phil Redmond, a local television producer. It was at its most popular in the 1980s and the early '90s and was known for its cutting-edge storylines. Huge ratings from the success of the 'body under the patio' and 'lesbian kiss' plots saw viewing levels peak at 9 million. The soap ended in 2003 after twenty-one years on air.

Desperate Scousewives first aired in 2011. It has been described as a 'dramality' – a show based on real people but with a loosely scripted plot and staged events. The series centres on several local characters with an emphasis on a group of heavily-tanned so-called glamorous circle of Scouse females and their day-to-day semi-fictional lives. After poor ratings in 2012, TV executives confirmed that it would not be recommissioned.

Websites

www.liverpool.com

www.visitliverpool.com

www.cityexplorerliverpool.co.uk

www.albertdock.com

www.echoarena.com

www.liverpoolmuseums.org.uk

www.tate.org.uk/liverpool

www.liverpoolfc.tv

www.evertonfc.com

www.liverpoolecho.co.uk

Things to do in Liverpool Checklist

Sample a bowl of hearty Scouse from one of the city's friendly cafés ☐

Visit the awe-inspiring Metropolitan and Anglican Cathedrals ☐

View some fabulous art at the Tate ☐

Take a wonderful tour of the city and its docks onboard the *Yellow Duck* ☐

Watch a thrilling football match featuring Liverpool or Everton – or even both ☐

Enjoy a few drinks in Liverpool's amazing bars and clubs ☐

Witness an evening's performance at one of the city's theatres or at the Echo Arena ☐

Ride the ferry across the Mersey ☐

Discover the wide selection of museums on offer such as the remarkable Museum of Liverpool ☐

Indulge in a shopping trip at the stores of Liverpool One ☐

Unusual Occasions

In 2008 Liverpool became the home of an enormous spider as part of its cultural celebrations. The 50ft arachnid, dubbed *La Machine*, clung onto the now demolished Concourse House outside of Lime Street Station before meandering through the crowds. It was constructed from steel and poplar wood with twelve human operators strapped to its frame. There were also fifty hydraulic axes of movement allowing the creature to scurry about at 2mph. Its visit was a grand people-pleaser but with its uncanny realism local onlooker Dorothy Wilson, eighty-two, fretfully told reporters at the time, 'I wouldn't like to meet it in the dark.'

To mark the *Titanic* centenary of April 2012, two giant puppets, a young girl and her diver uncle, roamed the city over a three-day excursion. Christened 'the Sea Odyssey', the event was organised by the French creative theatre specialists Royal De Luxe, who designed it to be magical tale of love, loss and reunion played out on a gigantic scale. It took place in many key city spaces, moving across North Liverpool and the city centre whilst wowing the hundreds of thousands of people who descended upon the city.

Victorian Liverpool

Picture Credits

71. A plaque in Campbell Square noting Charles Dickens' time as a special constable

73. A sign for the International Slavery Museum; the World Museum alongside the Liverpool Central Library

74. The Walker Art Gallery

75. The Bluecoat

77. The steps to Chavasse Park in Liverpool One; St John's Gardens

79. The Cains Brewery (David Humphreys)

81. The former White Star Headquarters

83. A photograph of William Gladstone; a statue of William Roscoe

85. A statue of Bessie Braddock in Lime Street Station

87. Portrait of Venus with planetary symbols, 1550; Kitty Wilkinson; X-Ray showing the bullet within the patient

89. Mary Ann Crawley in court; the court inside St George's Hall; nineteenth-century police (Brian Starkey)

91. Manchester man Duncan Owens committed suicide with poisoned beer; the Beehive where Mr Owens died

93. The pyramid tomb of William Mckenzie in the grounds of St Andrew's

95. Croxteth Hall

97. The blitzed-out interior of St Luke's church; Wood Street and Concert Square shown after bomb damage (Liverpool Record Office)

98. Carnage seen on the Strand (Liverpool Record Office)

99. A property in Clarence Street flattened during the Second World War (Liverpool Record Office)

101. Graduates celebrate on the steps of the cathedral (John Picton); His Holiness the Dali Llama (Luca Galuzzi), actress Kim Cattrall (George Pimental)

102. Liverpool seen from Everton Brow (Graham Maddrell)

103. A less scenic section of London Road

105. Crowds at a stage of the Matthew Street Festival; marchers of Liverpool Pride make their way through the town (Mike Hughes)

107. The Zutons (Marcelo Teson); The Wombats (Editor5807)

109. The Beatles wave to fans at John F. Kennedy International Airport

113. Giant TV screen in Liverpool

115. Lime Pictures (formerly Mersey Pictures) in Childwall. Shopping scenes for Brookside were once shot here. (Mikey)

117. Computer

119. A Mersey ferry sails to shore (Tony Sherratt)

121. The spider roams Liverpool

123. 'Sea Odyssey'

124. Lime Street; Liverpool from the Landing Stage

125. Ranelagh Street with a view of Central Station; Lord Street in 1900

***

For more Merseyside miscellany, visit Dan Longman's official Facebook page at **www.facebook.com/DanielKLongman** or follow him on Twitter at **www.Twitter.com/DanielKLongman**

If you enjoyed this book, you may also be interested in…

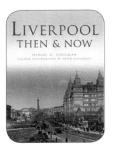

Liverpool Then & Now

DANIEL K. LONGMAN

Liverpool has a rich heritage, uniquely reflected in this new compilation. Contrasting a selection of forty-five archive images and forty-five full-colour modern photographs, this stunning collection explores the changing face of the city.

978 0 7524 5740 6

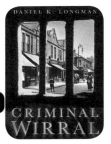

Criminal Wirral

DANIEL K. LONGMAN

Criminal Wirral is an intriguing and entertaining collection of some of the strangest, most despicable and comical crimes that took place on the Wirral peninsula throughout the Victorian era and the early twentieth century.

978 0 7509 4406 9

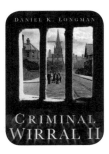

Criminal Wirral II

DANIEL K. LONGMAN

Read this sequel and uncover the grisly facts of what once lay floating in Birkenhead Park pond, a gruesome suicide on board a Woodside-bound locomotive and the farcical actions of a drunken butler one night at the stately Thurstaston Hall…

978 0 7524 5007 0

Visit our website and discover thousands of other History Press books.

www.thehistorypress.co.uk